D1278901

THE POWER OF
PRAISE

SEVEN HEBREW
WORDS FOR PRAISE

DAVID CHAPMAN

The Power of Praise:
7 Hebrew Words for Praise

David Chapman

Printed in the United States of America. All rights reserved under International Copyright Law. Contents and/or cover may not be reproduced in whole or in part in any form without the expressed written consent of the Publisher.

All Bible quotations are from the New King James Version unless otherwise noted.

Copyright © 2014

TRU Publishing
P.O. Box 201
Thatcher, Arizona 85552

Table of Contents

Introduction

There are several key Hebrew words in the Old Testament that are translated "praise," each having a unique and distinct meaning in the original language. In this small book, we will study the seven most prominent words and seek to put the Word of God into practice.

God is restoring again the Tabernacle of David in the last days, as prophesied in Amos 9:11 and Acts 15:16. Many churches are opening their hearts to a more expressive style of worship than ever before. In this material, we will discover the Biblical order of praise and worship.

The beautiful artwork on the cover and found within the book is used by permission from artist Carrie Todd. You can find her works at **mystudio13.com**.

Our Highest Calling

The believer's and the Church's highest calling is to worship God. When God created man, He breathed into him the breath of life. This life was not only physical life, but more importantly, spiritual life as well. When Adam sinned, he was cut off from the life of God... separated from communion with the Father. This created a God-shaped void in man that cannot be filled by anything else in this world.

Man searches but cannot find fulfillment outside of relationship with God. The void is always present. Conversely, when God breathed into Adam His very own life, there was a man-shaped "void" in God that only man can fill. For this reason, God seeks worshippers. He desires to spend time with His children and fill them with good things in His presence.

> **Psalm 16:11 In Your presence is fullness of joy; at Your right hand are pleasures forevermore.**

Praise and worship is not a drudgery for the child of God, but an exuberant encounter with a loving Father.

Psalm 100 outlines three important components to spending time in God's presence.

1. **Enter His gates with thanksgiving (v. 4)**
2. **Come into His courts with praise (v. 4)**
3. **Come before His presence with singing (v. 2)**

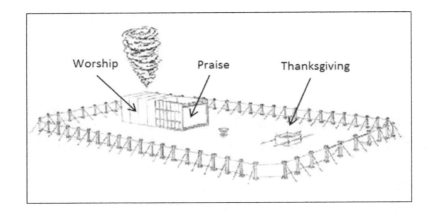

We must first enter with thanksgiving. An attitude of thankfulness and gratitude is required when coming before the King. There is no other way to make entry. As we begin to express our thankfulness, we move into praise within His courts. Praise is our response to all that He has done and all that we are believing that God will do in our lives.

Isaiah 61:3 says to "put on the garment of praise for the spirit of heaviness." Praise, active praise, will drive back the enemy. Psalm 22:3 says that God inhabits the praises of His people. As we praise Him, the presence of God is enthroned upon the praises of His people and we enter the highest crescendo, which is worship. Worship is our response to His presence.

Praise = our response to God's goodness
Worship = our response to God's presence

The Greatest Commandment

One day, the Pharisees decided to test Jesus by asking Him which was the greatest commandment in the law.

Matthew 22:34-38

34 But when the Pharisees heard that He had silenced the Sadducees, they gathered together.

35 Then one of them, a lawyer, asked Him a question, testing Him, and saying,

36 "Teacher, which is the great commandment in the law?"

37 Jesus said to him, "You shall love the Lord your God with all your heart, with all your soul, and with all your mind.

38 This is the first and great commandment."

Jesus said that the first and greatest commandment was to love the Lord your God with all your heart, with all your soul and with all your mind. This is the true essence of worship. The Pharisees understood religion, but Jesus was speaking to them about the language of the heart. God wants His people to express this kind of love for Him... to love the Lord with our entire being.

People often question what is the greatest sin? Is it murder? The love of money? Blasphemy? In fact, it is none of those things. If the greatest commandment is to love the Lord your God with all your heart, soul and mind, then by consequence, the greatest sin would be the failure to do so.

**The Greatest Sin = The Failure to Love the Lord
with All Your Heart, Soul & Mind**

Jesus went on to say, "And the second is like it: you shall love your neighbor as yourself." It is important to note that Jesus places this act of love for our fellow man second, after loving the Lord your God. It is clear that if we get our vertical relationship right that our horizontal ones will fall into alignment.

**First get the Vertical Relationship right and
the Horizontal ones will come into alignment**

But what does it really mean to love the Lord with all your heart, soul and mind? How can we do this and in what way do we demonstrate this love for Him? There are many man-made rules that religion has created over the centuries. Religion would have you to believe that if you keep these traditions of men then your requirement is fulfilled. However, Jesus was talking about the heart, that place that only God can touch, where true worship comes from. Listen to what Jesus said to the religious leaders of His day:

> **Matthew 15:8-9**
> **8 These people draw near to Me with their mouth, and honor Me with their lips, but their heart is far from Me.**
> **9 And in vain they worship Me, teaching as doctrines the commandments of men.**

The first occurrence of the word "worship" in the King James Bible is found in Genesis 22:5 when Abraham was commanded to offer up his only son to God.

Genesis 22

1 Now it came to pass after these things that God tested Abraham, and said to him, "Abraham!"And he said, "Here I am."

2 Then He said, "Take now your son, your only son Isaac, whom you love, and go to the land of Moriah, and offer him there as a burnt offering on one of the mountains of which I shall tell you."

3 So Abraham rose early in the morning and saddled his donkey, and took two of his young men with him, and Isaac his son; and he split the wood for the burnt offering, and arose and went to the place of which God had told him.

4 Then on the third day Abraham lifted his eyes and saw the place afar off.

5 And Abraham said to his young men, "Stay here with the donkey; <u>the lad and I will go yonder and worship</u>, and we will come back to you."

The seriousness of worship can clearly be seen in this first mention. The worship of the Living God is not some casual experience where you get a few goose bumps. It is not an emotional buzz you get because the music was especially good that day. It is a life-changing act of consecration and obedience. It means total surrender. In this first mention, it meant that Abraham was willing to offer back to God everything that he had lived for in the past 35 to 40 years.

Isaac meant everything to him. He was the fulfillment of God's promise in his life, but somewhere along the way, Abraham had turned Isaac into an idol. He was too consumed with the blessing and not the Blesser. And now God was requiring Abraham to give him back to Him.

> **Psalm 24:3-4**
> **3 Who may ascend into the hill of the Lord?**
> **Or who may stand in His holy place?**
> **4 He who has clean hands and a pure heart**
> **Who has not lifted up his soul to an idol...**

How often do we allow the many blessings from God in our lives to *detract* from our singular focus of worshipping Him? As we can see with Abraham, to worship God has cost... at the least it means death to self. God told Moses that no man can see Him and live (Exodus 33:20). Only dead men can see God.

> **Romans 12:1 I beseech you therefore, brethren, by the mercies of God, that you present your bodies a living sacrifice, holy, acceptable to God, which is your reasonable service.**

Seven Hebrew Words

With the importance of praise and worship in mind, we study the seven Hebrew words for praise. Though we may lift our hands or dance before Him as David did, if our hearts are far from Him then it is in vain that we worship.

The seven Hebrew words for "Praise" are as follows:

1. **HALAL:** "To shine, to boast, overwhelming excitement, to be clamorously foolish"
2. **YADAH:** "The extended hand"

3. **BARAK:** "To kneel in adoration, to bow"
4. **ZAMAR:** "To touch the strings, instrumental worship"
5. **SHABACH:** "To shout with triumph"
6. **TODAH:** "A confession, a sacrifice of thanksgiving"
7. **TEHILLAH:** "To sing the new song from the heart"

We will study each one of these forms of praise as in the pages ahead.

QUESTIONS

1. Explain why praise and worship is the highest calling of the believer:

2. Explain what the greatest commandment is and why:

3. Explain what the greatest sin is and why:

HALAL

"To shine, to boast, overwhelming excitement, to be clamorously foolish"

HALAL is translated as *praise* more than any other Hebrew word – 160 times in the Old Testament. The word "hallelujah" comes from this base word. It means "to shine, to boast, to demonstrate overwhelming excitement and to act clamorously foolish." Psalm 149 tells us that the Lord takes pleasure in His people when they HALAL His name with the dance.

Psalm 149:3-4

3 Let them praise [HALAL] His name with the dance;
Let them sing praises to Him with the timbrel and harp.
4 For the Lord takes pleasure in His people; He will
beautify the humble with salvation.

The Hebrew word for "beautify" in verse 4 is *paar* (pronounced paw-ar) and means "to adorn with glory." God wants to adorn His people with His glory when they HALAL His name. He will beautify, or adorn with glory, the humble. It takes humility and willingness to look like a fool in front of others in order to have the glory of God manifest upon you.

One cannot dwell on this thought too long before the story of David dancing before the Lord comes to mind. When Israel returned the Ark of the Covenant (signifying the presence and glory of God) back to Jerusalem, they brought it up with much fanfare.

David had previously tried to bring back the Ark, but failed to follow divine order. In the failed attempt, there was loud and beautiful music and a magnificent procession. However, they did not follow God's divine order. They put the Ark on a cart instead of the priests bearing it upon staves, according to the Law. As a result, God struck Uzzah dead as he reached to steady the Ark. That which is born of the flesh must be upheld by the flesh. The flesh cannot glorify God. This story can be found in 2 Samuel 6:1-10.

To HALAL is not simply a matter of playing music, dancing and singing. The divine order of the New Testament is to worship in spirit and in truth (John 4:23-24). I have been in services where the flesh was a stench in the nostrils of God.

There is a counterfeit to every genuine manifestation of God. The counterfeit to the divine order of worship is the emotional realm and the tradition of men. We cannot only worship God when we have the feeling to do so and we cannot worship according to the pattern of men. We must HALAL in the Spirit according to the Spirit of Truth.

> **John 4:23-24**
> **23 But the hour is coming, and now is, when the true worshipers will worship the Father in spirit and truth; for the Father is seeking such to worship Him.**
> **24 God is Spirit, and those who worship Him must worship in spirit and truth."**

When Jesus was having the conversation with the Samaritan woman at the well, she wanted to focus the discussion on the external components of "worship," such as where we should do it. But Jesus brought her back to the meaning of true worship.

Jesus said that true worshippers will worship the Father in spirit and truth. Religion always has a counterfeit to the things of God. These counterfeits never require the consecration of the heart, but instead focus on outward things. The counterfeit or substitute for spirit is emotion and the counterfeit for truth is tradition.

Divine Order of Worship	Counterfeit Worship
Spirit	Emotion
Truth	Tradition

The second time that David brought up the Ark (three months later), it was in accordance with God's divine order. David became the living definition of HALAL as he acted foolishly and danced before the Lord in front of all the people.

> **2 Samuel 6:14-15**
> **14 Then David danced before the Lord with all his might; and David was wearing a linen ephod.**
> **15 So David and all the house of Israel brought up the ark of the Lord with shouting and with the sound of the trumpet.**

David was not concerned with his dignity or his appearance as he danced before the Lord with all his might. I have found that being preoccupied with what other people think of you is the greatest inhibitor of enjoying God's presence and being adorned with His glory. There is a time and a place to just *let go and let God!* This is why David was called a man after God's own heart – his only concern was what God thought of him. Michal, his wife, watched him from the window and she despised him in her heart. When David got home that evening, Michal let him have it.

> **2 Samuel 6:16, 20**
> **16 Now as the ark of the Lord came into the City of David, Michal, Saul's daughter, looked through a window and saw King David leaping and whirling before the Lord; and she despised him in her heart.**
> **20 Then David returned to bless his household. And Michal the daughter of Saul came out to meet David,**

and said, "How glorious was the king of Israel today, uncovering himself today in the eyes of the maids of his servants, as one of the base fellows shamelessly uncovers himself!"

Michal was filled with such pride. She couldn't stand the idea of her husband/king acting so foolishly in front of the *little* people. David had the glory of God upon him and came home to bless his household. How sad that Michal missed out on what God was doing. Some churches are too concerned with their dignity to ever have a move of the Spirit and have God's glory revealed.

David's response to Michal was, basically, "You haven't seen anything yet!"

21 So David said to Michal, "It was before the Lord, who chose me instead of your father and all his house, to appoint me ruler over the people of the Lord, over Israel. Therefore I will play music before the Lord.
22 And I will be even more undignified than this, and will be humble in my own sight. But as for the maidservants of whom you have spoken, by them I will be held in honor."

As a result of her attitude, Michal was barren until the day of her death:

23 Therefore Michal the daughter of Saul had no children to the day of her death.

Churches that don't HALAL… don't demonstrate excitement for God, will eventually dry up and fail to re-produce.

I remember the first time that I danced before the Lord in public worship. I was just a young man, 22 years of age. I had been saved for two years and was attending a non-denominational Spirit-filled church. As we praised God that morning, I felt the prompting of the Holy Spirit that I had felt several times before. Previously, I didn't obey. I struggled with the idea of looking foolish before men.

This time, I wasn't going to let the Lord down. I shut my eyes and danced before the Lord with all my might. I opened my eyes and looked down and my feet hadn't budged! I learned on that day that when the Spirit moves on you in praise and worship that it still requires our physical obedience. I picked my feet up and danced and praised God. The Lord made known to me that He was pleased with both my obedience and my praise. What a blessing!

Today, I have no problem dancing before the Lord in praise. I still don't look good while I'm doing it, but it is beautiful to the Lord. That's all that I am concerned with.

Below are some other examples of the word being HALAL being used:

- Psalm 22:22 *I will declare Your name to My brethren; in the midst of the assembly I will praise [HALAL] You.*
- Psalm 35:18 *I will give You thanks in the great assembly; I will praise [HALAL] You among many people.*

- Psalm 107:32 *Let them exalt Him also in the assembly of the people, and praise [HALAL] Him in the company of the elders.*

As can be seen from the above Scriptures, God places emphasis on having a high level of excitement when praising Him in the congregation of the saints. God's House should be filled with exuberance when His people come together. Sometimes, God's people must be taught – both with the Word and by example – how to enter into God's presence. When I started the church that I pastor, it was a slow process to get people to enter into praise. There was lots of standing and looking around. But through teaching and setting the example, we have become a house of praise and worship and people are excited to praise God.

Further, when I started the church, we had no musicians or singers. We actually played worship videos on the screen. Praise and worship is not about music and it is not about feelings. It is about the presence of God. Now, we have lots of talented and anointed musicians and singers. But the focus remains on Him.

Too often, we allow our emotions to dictate whether we show excitement for God during the time of praise and worship. If we are down or discouraged we hold back from giving God the glory that is due Him.

Excitement and expectancy go hand in hand, and expectancy is the breeding ground for miracles. The time to shine and boast of God's goodness is BEFORE the answer to prayer, BEFORE the breakthrough, BEFORE the deliverance. Consider Israel when

19

God delivered them from Egypt. They did not believe God's Word nor sing His praise until the victory was manifest in the natural. As a consequence, they soon forgot all that God had done for them.

> **Psalm 106:10-15**
> **10 He saved them from the hand of him who hated them, and redeemed them from the hand of the enemy.**
> **11 The waters covered their enemies; There was not one of them left.**
> **12 <u>Then they believed His words</u>; They sang His praise.**
> **13 <u>They soon forgot His works</u>; They did not wait for His counsel,**
> **14 But lusted exceedingly in the wilderness, and tested God in the desert.**
> **15 And He gave them their request, but sent leanness into their soul.**

God still answered prayer for them, but there was leanness in their souls. The word "leanness" literally means a "wasting disease." The time to boast in God is when you are between a rock and a hard place, or as in Israel's case, when the Egyptian army is behind you and the Red Sea is in front of you.

Learning to praise God in times of difficulty is one of the greatest keys to living a victorious life as a believer. So many people get mad at God and quit when things get hard and it seems like prayer is going unanswered. They eventually come back to God, but much ground is forfeited by not being steadfast.

I want my life to be such that no one can tell when I am going through hard times and trials, at least not by looking at my praise and worship habits. When we HALAL before the Lord, we must learn to cast all of our cares upon Him! I love how the Amplified Bible translates 1 Peter 5:7:

> **Casting the whole of your care [all your anxieties, all your worries, all your concerns, once and for all] on Him, for He cares for you affectionately and cares about you watchfully.**

When we praise God, if we are preoccupied with anxieties, worries and concerns, we will be easily defeated. We are instructed to give them to God. I especially like how it says, "Once and for all." Too many times we give things to God and then take them back.

HALAL translated in the King James Bible as:

1. PRAISE: I Chron. 16:4; 23:5, 30; 25:3; II Chron. 8:14; 20:19, 21 (1st); 23:13; 29:30; 31:2; Ps. 22:22, 23, 26; 35:18; 56:4, 10 (both); 63:5; 69:30, 34; 74:21; 102:18; 104:35; 106:1, 48; 107:32; 111:1; 112:1; 113:1 (all); 113:9; 115:17, 18; 116:19; 117:1, 2; 119:164, 175; 135:1 (all), 3, 21; 145:2; 146:1 (both), 2 (1st), 10; 147:1 (1st), 12,20; 148: all; 149:1, 3, 9; 150; all; Jer. 20:13; 31:7; Joel 2:26
2. PRAISED: II Sam. 22:4; I Chron. 16:25, 36; 23:5; II Chron. 5:13; 7:6; 30:21; Ps. 18:3; 48:1; 96:4; 113:3; 145:3
3. PRAISES: II Chron. 29:30
4. PRAISING: II Chron. 5:13
5. GLORY: I Chron. 16:10; Ps. 105:3; 106:5; Is. 41:16; Jer. 4:2; 9:24
6. BOAST: Ps. 34:2; 44:8

QUESTIONS

1. Have I ever done HALAL during praise and worship? If not, why?

2. What are the benefits of HALAL?

3. List the ways that you can incorporate HALAL more into your personal and public praise:

YADAH

"The extended hand"

The Hebrew word YADAH comes from two root words. YAD, which means the open hand, direction, power and AH, which has reference to Jehovah. Together they are rendered Hands to God. In addition to *praise*, YADAH is also translated as *giving thanks* in the Old Testament. The word is found 114 times in the Old Testament.

Lifting our hands to God is a natural extension of our heart in our worship to God. Psalm 111:1 says, "I will praise [YADAH] the Lord with my whole heart, in the assembly of the upright and in the congregation."

Below are some additional examples of YADAH:

- Psalm 100:4 *Enter into His gates with thanksgiving, and into His courts with praise. Be thankful [YADAH] to Him, and bless His name.*
- Psalm 61:8 *So I will sing praise [YADAH] to your name forever, that I may daily perform my vows.*
- Psalm 28:7 *The Lord is my strength and my shield; my heart trusted in Him, and I am helped; therefore my heart greatly rejoices, and with my song I will praise [YADAH] Him.*

The Bible clearly instructs God's people to lift up their hands in praise and worship:

> **Psalm 134:2 Lift up your hands in the sanctuary, and bless the Lord.**

One may say, but that is the Old Testament; what does the New Testament have to say? The New Testament is just as clear:

> **I Timothy 2:8 I desire therefore that the men pray everywhere, lifting up holy hands.**

I remember a time as a new Christian when I was at a brother's home for a small prayer meeting. My brothers in the Lord were enjoying a great time of praise and I felt absolutely nothing. As I lifted my hands, I was struck with the condemnation that I didn't *feel* anything... I felt distant from God. I put my hands back down. I didn't want to be a hypocrite. As I put my hands down, the Spirit of God spoke to me and asked, "But do you *mean* it?" "Yes Lord," my heart cried out and I lifted my hands to the Lord and the feeling of distance soon lifted.

This is the pattern that David set forth in the book of Psalms. When discouraged, he would encourage himself by praising God. Yes, he kept it real, he didn't hold back any of his feelings leading up to when he praised God. But ultimately, he knew that expressing praise to God was the way to overcome discouragement. He didn't base it on a feeling, and at times, he literally spoke to his soul and commanded it to rise up and give God praise.

> **Psalm 42:5 Why are you cast down, O my soul? And why are you disquieted within me? Hope in God, for I shall yet praise [YADAH] Him For the help of His countenance.**

"I will YET praise [YADAH] Him." In other words, nothing that I go through will make me stop praising Him. Throughout the book of Psalms, although despair runs the deepest, praise ascends to the highest.

26

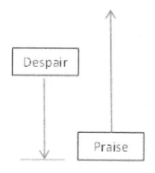

I have personally witnessed countless believers receive their deliverance as they lifted their hands before the Lord and praised Him, in spite of whatever they were going through. This is the "help of His countenance" as Psalm 42:5 so beautifully states. The Hebrew word for "countenance" means "the presence of His face."

Over the past 20 years or so, more and more denominational churches have become open to this expression of praise. I think that this is due to the emergence of contemporary worship music. God has used this medium to cross over denomination barriers. However, there are still some churches that are adamantly against this act of praise. Those who are, find themselves in opposition to the Word of God.

There are 39 specific verses in the Bible that deal with the lifting of hands in either praise or prayer.

Lifting hands to God is also an act of spiritual warfare. Remember when Israel was fighting against the Amalekites in the wilderness? When Moses, God's leader, raised his hands Israel prevailed, but when his hands dropped from being tired, Amalek prevailed.

Exodus 17:11-13

11 And so it was, when Moses held up his hand, that Israel prevailed; and when he let down his hand, Amalek prevailed.

12 But Moses' hands became heavy; so they took a stone and put it under him, and he sat on it. And Aaron and Hur supported his hands, one on one side, and the other on the other side; and his hands were steady until the going down of the sun.

13 So Joshua defeated Amalek and his people with the edge of the sword.

I do have a word of caution, however. We must guard against the lifting of hands becoming more about outward form than true praise. Years ago, I ran a television camera for a ministry. Sometimes the director would request a close-up of someone who was praising God. Upon first glance, it seemed an easy task; so many had their hands raised. But when I would zoom in for the close-up, I could see by the expression on their faces that they weren't truly praising God. They appeared bored or distracted. This is not the YADAH that the Bible talks about!

YADAH translated in the King James Bible as:

1. PRAISE: II Chron. 7:6, 20:21; Ps. 7:17, 9:1, 28:7, 30:9, 33:2, 42:5, 42:11, 43:4, 43:5, 44:8, 45:17, 49:18, 52:9, 54:6, 67:3, 67:55, 71:22, 76:10, 86:12, 88:10, 89:5, 99:3, 107:8, 15, 21, 31, 108:3, 109:30, 111:1, 118:19, 21, 28, 119:7, 138:2, 145:10; Is. 12:1
2. PRAISED: II Chron. 7:3
3. THANK: I Chron. 16:4, 7, 23:30, 29:13
4. THANKFUL: Ps. 100:4
5. THANKING: II Chron. 5:13
6. THANKS: II Sam. 22:50; I Chron. 16:8, 34, 35, 41, 25:3; II Chron. 31:2; Ezra 3:11; Neh. 12:24; Ps.6:5, 128:49, 30:4, 12, 35:18, 75:1, 79:13, 92:1, 97:12, 105:1, 106:147, 107:1, 118:1, 29, 119:62, 122:4, 136:1, 2, 3, 26, 140:131
7. THANKSGIVING: Neh. 11:17, 12:46

QUESTIONS

1. Have I ever done YADAH during praise and worship? If not, why?

2. What are the benefits of YADAH?

3. List the ways that you can incorporate YADAH more into your personal and public praise:

BARAK

"To kneel in adoration, to bow"

When we kneel or bow before the Lord, it is an act of humility. It is an expression of our devotion to our Heavenly Father. Abraham, Ezekiel, Daniel, Moses and others are recorded as worshipping by bowing or prostrating themselves before the Lord.

Psalm 95:6 Oh come, let us worship and bow down; let us kneel [BARAK] before the Lord our Maker.

There are times in the worship service when bowing down and kneeling is the only thing one can do. It is being overwhelmed by His presence to the point where you can no longer stand. The Greek word for "worship" in the New Testament is *proskuneo*; it is the word from which we get our English word *prostrate*.

Examples of kneeling, bowing, or falling prostrate before the Lord in worship:

- Exodus 34:8 *So Moses made haste and bowed his head toward the earth, and worshipped.*
- 2 Chronicles 5:13-14 *Indeed it came to pass, when the trumpeters and singers were as one, to make one sound to be heard in praising and thanking the Lord, and when they lifted up their voice with the trumpets and cymbals and instruments of music, and praised the Lord, saying: "For He is good, For His mercy endures forever," that the house, the house of the Lord, was filled with a cloud, so that the priests could not continue ministering because of the cloud; for the glory of the Lord filled the house of God.*
- Ephesians 3:14 *For this reason I bow my knees to the Father of our Lord Jesus Christ, 15 from whom the whole family in heaven and earth is named*
- Revelation 1:17 *And when I saw Him, I fell at His feet as dead. But He laid His right hand on me, saying to me, "Do not be afraid; I am the First and the Last."*

One of the greatest demonstrations of paying homage to God through kneeling is found in the book of Job. After losing absolutely everything Job was left alone, with nothing, just him and God. This is where Satan wanted to get Job. He was convinced that Job would turn his back on God. However, this is how Job responded:

> **Job 1:**
> **20 Then Job arose, tore his robe, and shaved his head; and he fell to the ground and worshipped.**
> **21 And he said:**
>
> **"Naked I came from my mother's womb, And naked shall I return there. The Lord gave, and the Lord has taken away; Blessed [BARAK] be the name of the Lord."**
> **22 In all this Job did not sin nor charge God with wrong.**

Job knelt before God after losing everything and gave praise to his Master. To kneel before the Lord is to acknowledge that although we may obtain many things in this life, we owe everything to Him.

It is interesting to read through the book of Job and conclude that in everything that Job went through, he never asked God to heal him. What Job wanted from God was to know WHY – "Why is all this happening to me God?" Most often, that is how we feel also when bad things happen. We get so consumed with the "why?" that the goodness of God gets clouded out.

Even though Job was never told by God why all those terrible things happened in his life, he never stopped praising God. BARAK is an act of surrender, yielding to God. When devastation comes against your life, the opportunity to praise God is a precious moment in time.

The Praise the Costs the Most Counts the Most

Through many trials in my own life, I have learned that when I have nothing left but God, I have enough to start over again. To BARAK is to make that total surrender in worship, often when it is the hardest.

Consider Jesus in the garden of Gethsemane. He prayed, in total surrender to the Father, "Not my will but Your will be done." He did this three times, while His disciples slept. The intensity of that moment was so severe that he sweated great drops of blood. In the end, He was surrendered to the Father's will.

Further, to BARAK is to kneel in adoration. It is so important to keep loving God during times of difficulty or pressure. In Daniel's day, when the king made a decree that no one should make any petitions except to the king, Daniel did not compromise. He continued to kneel before His God and make petition even though it meant possibly being thrown into the den of lions.

> **Daniel 6:10 Now when Daniel knew that the writing was signed, he went home. And in his upper room, with his windows open toward Jerusalem, he knelt down [BARAK] on his knees three times that day, and**

prayed and gave thanks before his God, as was his custom since early days.

Daniel did get thrown into the den of lions and God did deliver him. BARAK goes beyond an outward demonstration. It must come from the heart and represent total consecration. Consecration is something that is not spoken of too much in today's church. But God is looking for a people who are called unto Himself. A people who, if necessary, will respond like Daniel in a time of persecution.

In the days of King Jehosaphat, Israel was under attack from Ammon and Moab. The King didn't know what to do, but he turned to God (2 Chronicles 20:12). As he and the nation prayed, the Spirit of the Lord came upon Jahaziel and he prophesied that they should not be afraid, that the battle was not theirs, but God's (v 15). The Lord told them to stand and they would see the salvation of the Lord. In response Jehosaphat and all the people bowed before the Lord and worshipped Him.

2 Chronicles 20:17-18
17 You will not need to fight in this battle. Position yourselves, stand still and see the salvation of the Lord, who is with you, O Judah and Jerusalem!' Do not fear or be dismayed; tomorrow go out against them, for the Lord is with you."
18 And Jehoshaphat bowed his head with his face to the ground, and all Judah and the inhabitants of Jerusalem bowed before the Lord, worshipping the Lord.

In times of trouble when you don't know what to do, humble yourself before the Lord. Bow before Him in sincerity. The outcome had not occurred when they bowed in worship. They were trusting in a living God to fight their battles for them.

When kneeling before the Lord, do not busy your mind with what other people may think of you in a public setting such as church. Some may contend that no one should kneel in public, that Jesus said not to pray in front of others to be seen of men (Matthew 6:5). But Jesus was referring to the motive not the act. Our motive should not be to be seen by men. However, the Bible has many examples of public prayer and worship, including Jesus Himself on many occasions.

In addition to "kneel," BARAK is also translated "bless" and "blessed" in the Old Testament (KJV). The BARAK invokes the blessing of God.

BARAK is translated in the King James Bible as:

1. BLESS: Ps. 16:7; 66:8; 100:4; 103:1 (Both), 2, 20, 21, 22 (Both); 104:1, 35; 135:19 (Both); 135:20 (Both)
2. BLESSED: Ex. 18:10; Ruth 4:14; I Sam. 25:32,39; II Sam. 18:28; I Kings 1:48; 5:7; 8:15, 56; 10:9; I Chron. 16:36; II Chron. 2:12; 6:4; 9:8; 20:26; Ezra 7:27; Neh. 8:6; Ps. 18:46; 31:21; 41:13; 66:20; 68:19, 35; 72:18, 19; 89:52; 106:48; 119:12; 124:6; 135:21; 144:1; Ezek. 3:12; Dan. 2:20; 3:28; 4:34
3. KNEEL: Ps. 95:6

QUESTIONS

1. Have I ever done BARAK during praise and worship? If not, why?

2. What are the benefits of BARAK?

3. List the ways that you can incorporate BARAK more into your personal and public praise:

ZAMAR

"To touch the strings, instrumental worship"

ZAMAR is instrumental praise. It is used 41 times in the Bible. Music is a powerful tool to draw God's people into praise and worship. Throughout the hymnal of the Bible, the book of Psalms, music is presented in connection with praise and worship. There is great power in anointed music.

In the book of 1 Samuel, when King Saul would become troubled with a distressing spirit, David would come and play the harp in his presence and the distressing spirit would depart from Saul and he would be refreshed.

I Samuel 16

14 But the Spirit of the Lord departed from Saul, and a distressing spirit from the Lord troubled him.

15 And Saul's servants said to him, "Surely, a distressing spirit from God is troubling you.

16 Let our master now command your servants, who are before you, to seek out a man who is a skillful player on the harp. And it shall be that he will play it with his hand when the distressing spirit from God is upon you, and you shall be well."

17 So Saul said to his servants, "Provide me now a man who can play well, and bring him to me."

18 Then one of the servants answered and said, "Look, I have seen a son of Jesse the Bethlehemite, who is skillful in playing, a mighty man of valor, a man of war, prudent in speech, and a handsome person; and the Lord is with him."

19 Therefore Saul sent messengers to Jesse, and said, "Send me your son David, who is with the sheep."

20 And Jesse took a donkey loaded with bread, a skin of wine, and a young goat, and sent them by his son David to Saul.

21 So David came to Saul and stood before him. And he loved him greatly, and he became his armorbearer.

22 Then Saul sent to Jesse, saying, "Please let David stand before me, for he has found favor in my sight."

23 And so it was, whenever the spirit from God was upon Saul, that David would take a harp and play it with his hand. Then Saul would become refreshed and well, and the distressing spirit would depart from him.

When God's people come into the house of God and begin to praise Him with anointed music and singing, evil spirits that have been attacking the saints have to flee. There is a difference between anointed music that ushers in the presence of God and performance based music in the flesh. The latter has no ability to drive out demons and bring freedom.

We make war in the heavenlies and defeat the enemy through our praise and worship.

> **Psalm 144:1, 9**
> **1 Blessed be the Lord my Rock, Who trains my hands for war, and my fingers for battle.**
> **9 I will sing a new song to You, O God; on a harp of ten strings I will sing praises [ZAMAR] to You.**

I had a conversation not long ago with a veteran police officer who was also a strong believer. He told me that when he picked up someone who was belligerent and yelling profanities that he always turns on some praise music in the patrol car. He further told me that in all his years, without fail, the arrested person will stop and become silent. Praise God! What a testimony! As Christians we often fail to grasp the power that is at our disposal through praising God. This is the one thing that Satan hates. He was kicked out of heaven because we wanted God's worship instead of being the worshipper.

ZAMAR is true praise and not performance. In today's culture, the church tries to hard to compete with the world in the area of performance. I'm not saying that church musicians and singers should not be talented. Just the opposite, God's people are some of the most talented people on the earth. And God will increase one's talent when it is surrendered to Him. In fact, Scripture tells us that the singers and musicians that King David appointed were very skilled (2 Chronicles 34:12). But the focus of ZAMAR is not talent or performance. ZAMAR is praise to our God.

When the church comes together in one place and the praise and worship musicians and singers begin to play and sing, it is not their job to get the congregation to praise and worship. The focus of the praise team should be on ministering to the Lord. Whenever a praise team plays in effort to get a response from the congregation, it slips over into performance. The anointing will come as they worship God and play before an audience of One. The congregation will then respond to the presence of God.

There have been periods in church history when religion refused to allow music in the church. Bishop Gregory (A.D. 540-604) rejected congregational singing. He believed that singing was a function of the clergy. The Middle Ages (600-1517) were even worse. This period is known as the Dark Ages in church history. Musical instruments were completely ruled out of the church. Secular music developed during this period, but music in the church was dead. This was also a period of great spiritual captivity within the church. It wasn't until the Reformation Period that music was restored into the church.

The Dark Ages were much like the Babylonian Captivity of Israel under the Old Covenant.

> **Psalm 137:1-4**
> **1 By the rivers of Babylon, there we sat down, yea, we wept When we remembered Zion.**
> **2 We hung our harps Upon the willows in the midst of it.**
> **3 For there those who carried us away captive asked of us a song, and those who plundered us** *requested* **mirth,** *Saying,* **"Sing us** *one* **of the songs of Zion!"**
> **4 How shall we sing the Lord's song In a foreign land?**

The Lord's song was gone, but as Amos prophesied, the Lord built again the Tabernacle of David with musical praise and worship in the end times. We will talk more about this in the chapter on the Tabernacle of David.

The Prophetic Anointing
Anointed music also has the ability to clothe the man of God with the prophetic mantle.

> **2 Kings 3:12-16**
> **12 And Jehoshaphat said, "The word of the Lord is with him." So the king of Israel and Jehoshaphat and the king of Edom went down to him.**
> **13 Then Elisha said to the king of Israel, "What have I to do with you? Go to the prophets of your father and the**

prophets of your mother." But the king of Israel said to him, "No, for the Lord has called these three kings together to deliver them into the hand of Moab."

14 And Elisha said, "As the Lord of hosts lives, before whom I stand, surely were it not that I regard the presence of Jehoshaphat king of Judah, I would not look at you, nor see you.

<u>15 But now bring me a musician." Then it happened, when the musician played, that the hand of the Lord came upon him.</u>

16 And he said, "Thus says the Lord..."

Until the musician came (KJV uses "minstrel"), Elisha did not have the unction to prophesy. The Hebrew word for "musician" here is *nagan* (naw-gan) and means, "To play, and sing along with, a stringed instrument." As the musician or minstrel played and sang, the hand of the Lord came Elisha to speak prophetically. Although this is the only instance of this that was recorded, it seems clear that this was nothing out of the ordinary.

The praise and worship ministry has a huge impact on the delivery of the Word of God. ZAMAR before the Lord stirs up the prophetic gifting and releases the anointing of God. There is a passage of Scripture in Paul's first letter to Corinth that describes the atmosphere where the prophetic is flowing.

1 Corinthians 14:24-26
24 But if all prophesy, and an unbeliever or an uninformed person comes in, he is convinced by all, he is convicted by all.

25 And thus the secrets of his heart are revealed; and so, falling down on *his* face, he will worship God and report that God is truly among you.

26 How is it then, brethren? Whenever you come together, each of you has a psalm, has a teaching, has a tongue, has a revelation, has an interpretation. Let all things be done for edification.

When the prophetic anointing is in the room and those with that mantle begin to flow, the secrets of men's hearts are revealed and godly repentance occurs. The stage is set for the move of the Spirit, in large part, because of the anointed ZAMAR – the ministry of the minstrel.

Further, in verse 26, Paul speaks of the psalm when the church comes together. Along with teaching, tongues, revelations and interpretations, he says that it is for the purpose of edification.

The Psalmist

King David was many things during his lifetime. Chiefly, he was a man after God's own heart. He was a warrior, King of God's people, prophet and writer of divine Scripture. But in his dying days, the title of Psalmist was used to describe him. A psalmist is a composer of songs or psalms. Over half of the 150 psalms in the book of Psalms are ascribed to David.

> **2 Samuel 23:1**
> **Now these are the last words of David.**
> **Thus says David the son of Jesse;**
> **Thus says the man raised up on high,**
> **The anointed of the God of Jacob,**

And the sweet psalmist of Israel

By the end of his reign, David had built an orchestra composed of 4,000 Levite musicians (I Chronicles 23:1-5). Of these, 288 were specifically anointed as psalmists (I Chronicles 25:2-7).

Moses and Miriam are also great examples of leaders who were also anointed psalmists. There are many great psalmists in the body of Christ today. God is raising up anointed and skilled composers of worship, straight from the throne of God.

The Counterfeit: Satan and Music

It is important to understand the background of Satan. As Lucifer, he was the original worship leader and music director in Heaven before he was lifted up with pride and fell. Ezekiel chapter 28 tells us that he was the Anointed Cherub and that tambourines were created within his body.

> **Ezekiel 28:13-14 (KJV)**
> **13 ...The workmanship of thy tabrets [tambourines] and of thy pipes was prepared in thee in the day that thou wast created.**
> **14 Thou art the anointed cherub that covereth;**

Lucifer was the worshiper but wanted to be the one worshipped. God kicked him out of heaven. Since his fall, Satan has used the power of music to divert worship from the true God to himself.

Satan's influence on music over the years is unmistakable. Through it, he captures the hearts and minds of young people.

Rebellion to God is the central message. Many studies have demonstrated that heavy rock music causes emotional and behavioral disorders.

Hypocrisy and Music

God takes no delight in "worship" offered to Him in the form of music when the people's hearts are filled with hypocrisy. God demands a pure heart from those who minister to Him in music and lead God's people in praise and worship. In Amos, we read that God despised the temple music because of the condition of the people's hearts.

> **Amos 5:21, 23**
> **21 I hate, I despise your feast days, and I do not savor your sacred assemblies.**
> **23 Take away from Me the noise of your songs, for I will not hear the melody of your stringed instruments.**

Psalm 150, the last psalm on God's song book, makes it clear that we are to praise God with music.

> **Psalm 150**
> **3 Praise Him with the sound of the trumpet;**
> **Praise Him with the lute and harp!**
> **4 Praise Him with the timbrel and dance;**
> **Praise Him with stringed instruments and flutes!**
> **5 Praise Him with loud cymbals;**
> **Praise Him with clashing cymbals!**

While there are not specific references to musical instruments in the New Testament church, it must be remembered that not everything was recorded. Further, the Old Testament was the only Bible that the early church had, including the book of Psalms – God's songbook.

Most importantly, when we get to the book of Revelation in the New Testament, we see through John's visions, that music is a big part of heaven's worship.

> **Revelation 14:2-3**
> **2 And I heard a voice from heaven, like the voice of many waters, and like the voice of loud thunder. And I heard the sound of harpists playing their harps.**
> **3 They sang as it were a new song before the throne…**

May God's will be done on earth just as it is in heaven!

ZAMAR translated in the King James Bible as:

1. PRAISE: Ps. 57:7; 108:1; 138:1
2. SING PRAISES: Ps. 9:11; 18:49; 27:6; 47:6 (all), 7; 92:1; 108:3; 135:3; 144:9; 146:2; 147:1; 149:3
3. SING: Ps. 30:4, 12; 33:2; 57:9; 59:17; 61:8; 66:2, 4 (both); 71:22, 23; 75:9; 98:4, 5; Isa. 12:5
4. SING PSALMS: Ps. 105:2

QUESTIONS

1. Have I ever done ZAMAR during praise and worship? If not, why?

2. What are the benefits of ZAMAR?

3. List the ways that you can incorporate ZAMAR more into your personal and public praise:

SHABAC

"To shout with triumph"

SHABACH means to shout to the Lord with the voice of triumph! Psalm 63:3 says, *Because Your lovingkindness is better than life, My lips shall praise [SHABACH] You.* There are times to be still before the Lord and there are times to shout unto the Lord. Both have their proper place in our praise and worship. The purpose of a shout is not to draw attention to one's self, but to magnify God.

...n of the word SHABACH means to shout to ...he voice of triumph. Triumph is a fantastic word ...v Testament. Some have mistakenly taken it to be ...ymous with "victory." However, this is not the case. The ...tory is won on the battle field, or in the case of Christianity, on the Cross. Triumph is the parade that occurs *after* the victory. First, Jesus triumphed over the devil and now, every believer may triumph in the face of adversity, by praising God.

> **Colossians 2:14-15**
> **14 Having wiped out the handwriting of requirements that was against us, which was contrary to us. And He [Jesus] has taken it out of the way, having nailed it to the cross.**
> **15 Having disarmed principalities and powers, He made a public spectacle of them, triumphing over them in it.**

> **2 Corinthians 2:14 Now thanks be to God who always leads us in triumph in Christ**

Through the Blood of the Cross, Jesus disarmed the devil and made a public spectacle of him. He humiliated him openly with the parade of all parades, as Jesus carried His Own blood into the Holy of Holies in Heaven. Conversely, every time a believer shouts unto God and pleads the Blood of Jesus, the devil, once again is put to open shame.

> **Psalm 47:1 Oh, clap your hands, all you peoples! Shout [SHABACH] to God with the voice of triumph!**

Shouting releases great energy in the spirit realm. The forces of spiritual joy are released into the heavens. God is certainly not hard of hearing, but neither is He nervous! Some believers are so tightly wound that it would do them well to release a shout unto the Lord.

When Israel was entering the Promised Land, the walls of Jericho stood between them and the land of Canaan. God gave Joshua, what appeared to be some foolish instructions (Joshua 6:3-5):

1. March around the city once a day for six days, with the Ark of God leading the way.
2. On the seventh day, march around the city seven times.
3. The priests are to blow their trumpets (seven trumpets).
4. Upon hearing the trumpets, all of the people are to shout with a great shout.
5. The wall of the city will fall down flat.

When the people did exactly what God instructed, the walls came down when Israel shouted. This wall, as archaeologists have uncovered, was about 17 feet high and about 5 feet thick. When the people of God shouted, the wall didn't just fall over. Excavations have shown that the wall was literally pushed into the ground! A truly awesome miracle of God – brought on by obedience to the Lord.

Below are some additional examples of SHABACH:

- Isaiah 12:6 *Cry out and shout [SHABACH], O inhabitant of Zion, for great is the Holy One of Israel in your midst!"*
- Psalm 35:27 *Let them shout [SHABACH] for joy and be glad, who favor my righteous cause; and let them say continually, "Let the Lord be magnified, who has pleasure in the prosperity of His servant."*
- Psalm 32:11 *Be glad in the Lord and rejoice, you righteous; and shout for joy, all you upright in heart!*

There have been times in my life when the SHABACH has been the catalyst for breakthrough in the spirit. It is not the loudness of the shout that contains the power, but the anointing of the Holy Spirit.

Zechariah 4:6 Not by might nor by power, but by My Spirit, Says the Lord of hosts.

In the book of Ezra, when they laid the foundation of the temple, they praised the Lord and shouted with a loud and joyful shout:

Ezra 3:10-13
10 When the builders laid the foundation of the temple of the Lord, the priests stood in their apparel with trumpets, and the Levites, the sons of Asaph, with cymbals, to praise [HALAL] the Lord, according to the ordinance of David king of Israel.
11 And they sang responsively, praising [HALAL] and giving thanks [YADAH] to the Lord:

54

"For He is good,

For His mercy endures forever toward Israel."

Then all the people shouted with a great shout, when they praised the Lord, because the foundation of the house of the Lord was laid.

12 But many of the priests and Levites and heads of the fathers' houses, old men who had seen the first temple, wept with a loud voice when the foundation of this temple was laid before their eyes. Yet many shouted aloud for joy,

13 so that the people could not discern the noise of the shout of joy from the noise of the weeping of the people, for the people shouted with a loud shout, and the sound was heard afar off.

SHABACH is also translated "still" in Psalm 65:7 and 89:9. God stills the waves of the sea with SHABACH. Sometimes when you want to shut the lies of the devil, you need to shout unto the Lord.

Pentecostals have long been famous for shouting to the Lord during praise. The more modern Spirit-filled churches have shied away from this activity. It can appear to be undignified. But God chooses the foolish things to confound the wise.

SHABACH translated in the King James Bible as:

1. COMMEND: Eccl. 8:15
2. GLORY: 1 Chron. 16:35
3. KEEP IT IN: Pr. 29:11
4. PRAISE: Ps. 63:3; 117:1; 145:4; 147:12; Eccl. 4:2
5. STILL: Ps. 65:7; 89:9
6. TRIUMPH: Ps. 106:47

QUESTIONS

1. Have I ever done SHABACH during praise and worship? If not, why?

2. What are the benefits of SHABACH?

3. List the ways that you can incorporate SHABACH more into your personal and public praise:

TODAH

"A confession, a sacrifice of thanksgiving"

TODAH comes from the same root word as YADAH, which means "the extended hand." But TODAH also conveys the "confession of our lips" and "thanksgiving to God."

Jesus said that out of the abundance of the heart the mouth speaks (Luke 6:45). God is looking for a thankful heart. As we previously discussed, there is great importance upon entering into His gates with thanksgiving. There is no other way to enter.

Psalm 100:

1. **Enter His gates with Thanksgiving**
2. **Come into His courts with Praise**
3. **Come before His presence with Singing**

When you study out the use of the word TODAH, it becomes clear that it greatly involves thanking God for things *not yet received*. Over the years, as a pastor, I have observed that when a believer is defeated, there is usually a problem with his confession. It is important to train our thinking and our confession to line up to the Word of God.

Some may try to label this as "name it and claim it." That's an easy way out to avoid what the Word of God says about this important matter of confession. Here are just a handful of verses about the power of the tongue:

- Proverbs 18:21
- Proverbs 12:18
- Proverbs 15:4
- Psalm 19:14
- Ephesians 4:29
- Mark 11:23
- Luke 6:45

I experienced some health issues not long ago and had a minor procedure done. There were some post-operative complications as a result. I have always been very healthy and this was new territory for me. I prayed and prayed, asking God to deliver me from these issues. Yet the problems persisted and I had to go to the emergency room on eight different occasions. I ended up seeing a specialist several times. In the process, every day, I would fight the temptation to get in fear. I would do this by confessing God's Word instead of the thoughts of fear and worry that would attack my mind.

After several weeks, the chief specialist advised me that he wanted to operate. I told him that I was not going to do that. By this time, I had a conviction that God was going to deliver me out of the problem. I went home from the doctor's office and got up the next morning healed. I know that if I had bought into the fears and confessed the worst that I would not have been healed.

How can I say that I would not have been healed if I had confessed fear and doubt? The Word of God is very blunt about this subject.

> **James 1:6-8**
> **6 But let him ask in faith, with no doubting, for he who doubts is like a wave of the sea driven and tossed by the wind.**
> **7 For let not that man suppose that he will receive anything from the Lord;**
> **8 he is a double-minded man, unstable in all his ways.**

So, if we doubt, we will not receive *anything* from the Lord. That's God's Word – not mine. And we cannot believe in our hearts and speak fear and doubt with our mouth. Jesus said that out of the abundance of the heart the mouth would speak (Matthew 12:34).

The best recipe for the offering of thanksgiving is found in Philippians chapter four:

> **Philippians 4:6-7**
> **6 Be anxious for nothing, but in everything by prayer and supplication, with thanksgiving, let your requests be made known to God;**
> **7 and the peace of God, which surpasses all understanding, will guard your hearts and minds through Christ Jesus.**

Here are the steps that Paul outlined:

1. Don't be anxious
2. Prayer and supplication
3. Thanksgiving
4. God's peace
5. Right meditation (v 8)

Point 2 mentions prayer *and* supplication. Supplication differs from general prayer, in that supplication is a specific request for yourself. A *petition* is also a specific request, but is generally for someone else. Supplication is a prayer need for something specific in your life. This is why it's important not to be anxious and worry.

After putting things before the Lord in prayer and supplication, the next thing we should do is offer thanksgiving for the answer – before we see it in the natural. It is easy to thank God *after* we see the answer. But this leads to leanness in our soul (Psalm 106:15).

The original Greek word for "thanksgiving" in verse 6 is *eucharistia*, which means, "actively speaking thanks and gratitude to God." The word is in the present tense, meaning that it should be a habitual practice. TODAH should become part of our nature. "In all things give thanks" it says in 1 Thessalonians 5:18.

Consider Abraham. He stood on the promise and believed God for 25 years for a son. After 10 years though, he thought he would "help God out." That work of the flesh produced Ishmael, from which the Arab nations arose. They are still a thorn in Israel's side today. That which is born of the flesh is flesh! From this, Abraham learned a great lesson. No matter what things look like in the natural, if God promised you something, have faith in God and thank Him for the answer.

> **Romans 4:18-20**
> **18 who, contrary to hope, in hope believed, so that he became the father of many nations, according to what was spoken, "So shall your descendants be."**
> **19 And not being weak in faith, he did not consider his own body, already dead (since he was about a hundred years old), and the deadness of Sarah's womb.**

20 He did not waver at the promise of God through unbelief, but was strengthened in faith, giving glory to God

Abraham learned to give glory to God even when it didn't look like it was going to happen. Contrary to hope, in hope he believed. Bible hope is a *cheerful, confident expectancy.* TODAH became a way of life for Abraham, as it must be for us if we are to receive the answer of the promise.

Listed below are some other examples of TODAH in Scripture:

- Psalm 50:23 Whoever offers praise [TODAH] glorifies Me; and to him who orders his conduct aright, I will show the salvation of God.
- Jeremiah 33:11 The voice of joy and the voice of gladness, the voice of the bridegroom and the voice of the bride, the voice of those who will say: "Praise [YADAH] the Lord of hosts, for the Lord is good, for His mercy endures forever"— and of those who will bring the sacrifice of praise [TODAH] into the house of the Lord. For I will cause the captives of the land to return as at the first,' says the Lord.

One of my favorite psalms is Psalm 42 because it speaks of thirsting for God even though your life is in turmoil. In this psalm, we are told to both to TODAH and to YADAH to help bring us up out of the depths of despair.

Psalm 42:1-5
1 As the deer pants for the water brooks,

So pants my soul for You, O God.
2 My soul thirsts for God, for the living God.
When shall I come and appear before God?
3 My tears have been my food day and night,
While they continually say to me,
"Where is your God?"
4 When I remember these things,
I pour out my soul within me.
For I used to go with the multitude;
I went with them to the house of God,
With the voice of joy and praise [TODAH],
With a multitude that kept a pilgrim feast.
5 Why are you cast down, O my soul?
And why are you disquieted within me?
Hope in God, for I shall yet praise [YADAH] Him
For the help of His countenance.

When life brings you to the bottom and tears become a constant, pour out your soul to God and change your confession to one of praise to God for that which has not been received yet.

TODAH translated in the King James Bible as:

1. THANK: II Chron. 29:31 (Both); 33:16
2. THANKS: Neh. 12:31, 38, 40
3. THANKSGIVING: Lev. 22:29; Ps. 26:7, 50:14, 69:30, 95:2, 107:22, 116:17, 147:7; Isa. 51:3; Jer.30:19; Amos 4:5; Jonah 2:9
4. PRAISE: Ps. 42:4, 50:23; Jer. 17:26; 33:11
5. PRAISES: Ps. 56:12, 68:4, 32; 75:9
6. CONFESSION: Josh. 7:19; Ezra 10:11

QUESTIONS

1. Have I ever done TODAH during praise and worship? If not, why?

2. What are the benefits of TODAH?

3. List the ways that you can incorporate TODAH more into your personal and public praise:

TEHILLAH

"To sing the new song from the heart"

TEHILLAH means to sing the new song from the heart. The new song is often born in adversity. When the devil thinks he has you cornered and there's no way out, the Spirit of God will birth in you a new song of praise unto our God. And praise will defeat the enemy!

David understood the power of the new song when God delivered out of the horrible pit:

Psalm 40:2-3
2 He also brought me up out of a horrible pit,
Out of the miry clay,
And set my feet upon a rock,
And established my steps.
3 He has put a new song in my mouth—
Praise [TEHILLAH] to our God;

The world doesn't understand it, but when God delivers you, He places a new song in your heart that wants to praise God. You remember from whence He has brought you and cannot help but to sing His praises. I remember when I was first saved. Like David, He brought me up out of a horrible pit. My pit was one of depression and drug abuse. After God saved and delivered me, the grass seemed greener, the sky seemed bluer, the air smelled fresher. I was alive! I was once dead in my trespasses and sins, but God brought me up out of the pit and set my feet upon a rock! He put a new song in my mouth and I wanted to praise Him continuously.

Another example of God birthing a new song in your life when everything seems to be falling apart is found in Isaiah 61. Here, the Bible addresses how to respond to the spirit of heaviness. The Hebrew word for "heaviness" is *keheh* and it means, "weak, dark, despondent."

Isaiah 61:3
To console those who mourn in Zion,
To give them beauty for ashes,
The oil of joy for mourning,

The garment of praise [TEHILLAH] for the spirit of
heaviness;
That they may be called trees of righteousness,
The planting of the Lord, that He may be glorified.

The only way to combat the spirit of heaviness is to choose to
put on the garment of praise – TEHILLAH – and begin to sing the
new song from up out of your spirit!

Depression is such a huge problem in today's world.
Healthline.com reports that currently 121 million people around
the world are suffering from serious depression. In the United
States it is even worse. Approximately one in every ten
Americans suffer from depression. Sadly, that number increases
by about 20% every year.

This is not factoring in those who have occasional bouts with
depression. The spirit of heaviness can try to attack even the
most jovial individual. TEHILLAH is one of the strongest forces to
overcome this spirit. But, as Isaiah 61 tells us, we must put it on!
TEHILLAH is *not* a feeling, an emotion; it is a force of the spirit.
Anyone can sing a new song when things are great. But the Holy
Spirit is able to birth in us a new song even when times are the
hardest and we feel like giving up in the natural.

For there to be new life there must first be a death. God allows
you to be brought to the end of yourself (i.e., death) in order to
raise you back up in His power with a new song in your heart.
The experience of this transformation is something you can't
learn from a book or a sermon.

The New Testament also speaks of praising God with the new song, the spiritual song:

> **Colossians 3:16-17**
> **16 Let the word of Christ dwell in you richly in all wisdom, teaching and admonishing one another in psalms and hymns and spiritual songs, singing with grace in your hearts to the Lord.**
> **17 And whatever you do in word or deed, do all in the name of the Lord Jesus, giving thanks to God the Father through Him.**

> **Ephesians 5:18-20**
> **18 And do not be drunk with wine, in which is dissipation; but be filled with the Spirit,**
> **19 speaking to one another in psalms and hymns and spiritual songs, singing and making melody in your heart to the Lord,**
> **20 giving thanks always for all things to God the Father in the name of our Lord Jesus Christ.**

From these two passages we can draw the following conclusions:

1. Let the Word of God speak into your life
2. Be filled with the Holy Spirit
3. Sing psalms, hymns and spiritual songs – making melody in your heart
4. Always give thanks to God the Father

Below are some other examples of the word TEHILLAH:

- Psalm 22:3 *But You are holy, enthroned in the praises [TEHILLAH] of Israel.*
- 2 Chronicles 20:22 *Now when they began to sing and to praise [TEHILLAH], the Lord set ambushes against the people of Ammon, Moab, and Mount Seir, who had come against Judah; and they were defeated.*
- Psalm 34:1 *I will bless the Lord at all times; His praise [TEHILLAH] shall continually be in my mouth.*

God inhabits, or is enthroned upon the praises – the new song from the heart – of His people. What a beautiful picture! This Hebrew word also means, "to marry." This reminds me of the marriage supper of the Lamb. A beautiful new song will be sung on that day when the bride has been made ready for the Lamb.

Revelation 19:6-9
6 And I heard, as it were, the voice of a great multitude, as the sound of many waters and as the sound of mighty thunderings, saying, "Alleluia! For the Lord God Omnipotent reigns!
7 Let us be glad and rejoice and give Him glory, for the marriage of the Lamb has come, and His wife has made herself ready."
8 And to her it was granted to be arrayed in fine linen, clean and bright, for the fine linen is the righteous acts of the saints.
9 Then he said to me, "Write: 'Blessed are those who are called to the marriage supper of the Lamb!'" And he said to me, "These are the true sayings of God."

The new song is sung because we are in love with the Bridegroom. Jesus is worthy of our adoration and affection. As we praise Him, a beautiful adornment comes upon us.

TEHILLAH is translated in the King James Bible as:

PRAISE: I Chron. 16:35; II Chron. 20:22; Neh. 9:5; 12:46; Ps. 9:14; 22:3, 25; 33:1; 34:1; 35:28; 40:3; 48:10; 51:15; 65:1; 66:2, 8; 71:6, 8, 14; 79:13; 100:4; 102:21; 106:2, 12, 47; 111:10; 119:171; 145: Title, 21; 147:1 (2nd); 148:14 (1st); 149:1 (2nd).

QUESTIONS

1. Have I ever done TEHILLAH during praise and worship? If not, why?

2. What are the benefits of TEHILLAH?

3. List the ways that you can incorporate TEHILLAH more into your personal and public praise:

The Tabernacle of David

Amos 9:11 On that day I will raise up The tabernacle of David, which has fallen down, and repair its damages; I will raise up its ruins, And rebuild it as in the days of old

Acts 15:15-16
15 And with this the words of the prophets agree, just as it is written:
16 After this I will return And will rebuild the tabernacle of David, which has fallen down; I will rebuild its ruins, and I will set it up.

The prophet Amos prophesies about a day in the future when God will restore the Tabernacle of David. About 800 years later, James quotes the promise and applies it to the church age. How could a tent (i.e., David's tabernacle) from 3,000 years ago have any impact on the church today? First, there was an immediate application in the book of Acts of the conversion of the Gentiles into the church.

But, as it relates to our subject we will find out the following:

- There is a divine order to worship
- There are consequences when we fail to follow divine order to worship
- Religion, outside of divine order, will continue until Jesus returns
- All of the expression of the seven Hebrew words for "praise" is found in the Tabernacle of David

75

- God is restoring the full expression of praise and worship to the Church

The Ark of the Covenant
The Ark of the Covenant was the only piece of furniture in the Tabernacle of David. The Ark was the central figure in all of God's dealings with the nation of Israel. There are 185 references to the Ark in the Old Testament.

- The Ark was 45 inches in length and 27 inches in width and height (Exodus 25:10).
- The Ark was made of shittim wood, symbolizing humanity and overlaid with gold, symbolizing deity (Exodus 25:11). Thus, the Ark perfectly typified Christ – the God-Man.
- The Ark contained the tables of the Law, the golden pot of manna and Aaron's rod that budded (Hebrews 9:4).
- The Ark was housed in the Holy of Holies in the Tabernacle of Moses, and later, Solomon's Temple.
- The High Priest entered the Holy of Holies once per year on the Day of Atonement and sprinkled the blood of the animal sacrifice upon the Mercy Seat that covered the Ark, for the atonement of the sins of Israel (Leviticus 16).

The Ark of God represented:

- The Throne of God
- The Presence of God
- The Fullness of God
- The Glory of God

The above is summed up in the Shekinah Glory of God!

The study of the word for God's presence – its origin and history brings us to the Hebrew word Sh'cheenah or as we pronounce it Shekinah. God's people frequently used the term Shekinah interchangeably with the Word God. In the Jewish mind it always spoke of the fact that He "dwelt in" or "rested upon" those who merited His favor, whether an individual, a community, or the entire Jewish people.

> **Exodus 25:22 And there I will meet with you, and I will speak with you from above the mercy seat, from between the two cherubim which are on the ark of the Testimony, about everything which I will give you in commandment to the children of Israel.**

In praise and worship, the apex is to have an encounter with the living God. His presence is now manifest when His people come before Him in adoration.

As it relates to the story of David bringing back the Ark from the Philistine captivity, divine order for the transit of the Ark, as prescribed by God, needs to be understood.

- The Ark was to be covered with a Covering Veil of badger's skins and blue cloth.
- The Ark had four rings of gold, two per side. Staves (wood overlaid with gold) were to be driven through the rings when transported.
- The Ark was to be transported by the priests, specifically Kohathites of the tribe of Levi, using the staves to carry it upon their shoulders.
- There was to be NO HUMAN CONTACT.

Israel would carry the Ark before them as they went into battle. It was there when the walls of Jericho came down. Israel could not be defeated when the presence of God was with them. But somewhere along the way, it became more about the superstition than the glory. Israel thought that they could rebel against God's commands, but manipulate victory through the Ark. This is a lesson for God's people. We do not praise Him in order to *get something* from Him. We cannot live like the world and use praise as some token to get God's blessing!

This was the case in Israel when the Philistines captured the Ark.

The Captivity of the Ark – Ichabod

When we look at the captivity of the Ark, we must first understand why God allowed the Ark to be taken captive.

> **1 Samuel 2:12 Now the sons of Eli were corrupt; they did not know the Lord.**

Hophni and Phinehas were engaging in illicit behavior, such as appropriating the best portion of sacrifices for themselves, and having sexual relations with the women who were serving in the sanctuary.

There is only so long that God will tolerate sin in His house. His glory and rebellion cannot coexist.

> **1 Samuel 4:17-18, 21-22**
> **17 So the messenger answered and said, "Israel has fled before the Philistines, and there has been a great**

slaughter among the people. Also your two sons, Hophni and Phinehas, are dead; and the ark of God has been captured."

18 Then it happened, when he made mention of the ark of God, that Eli fell off the seat backward by the side of the gate; and his neck was broken and he died, for the man was old and heavy. And he had judged Israel forty years.

Phineas' wife had a baby after his death:

21 Then she named the child Ichabod, saying, "The glory has departed from Israel!" because the ark of God had been captured and because of her father-in-law and her husband. 22 And she said, "The glory has departed from Israel, for the ark of God has been captured."

After seven months of God's wrath upon the Philistines (God gave them hemorrhoids everywhere the Ark was kept), the Philistines surrendered the Ark back to Israel (1 Samuel 6:1-3). The men of Kirjath-Jearim retrieved the Ark and brought it to Abinadab's house. It remained there for 20 years.

1 Samuel 7:2 So it was that the ark remained in Kirjath Jearim a long time; it was there twenty years. And all the house of Israel lamented after the Lord.

All of Israel lamented because the glory of God had departed.

King David

God put it into the heart of David to restore God's glory to His people. David was a man after God's own heart.

Acts 13:22 And when He had removed him, He raised up for them David as king, to whom also He gave testimony and said, 'I have found David the son of Jesse, a man after My own heart, who will do all My will.'

David was the youngest son of Jesse and the last one from Jesse's household to be considered as king. Samuel thought the several of his older brothers would be more suitable, but God told Samuel that He does not look on someone as man does – by the outer appearance, but that He looks on the heart (1 Samuel 16:7).

David was the only leader of Israel to have a perfect military record – he was undefeated in battle. In addition to being a man of war, David was a worshipper. He wrote approximately half of the Psalms. Some of the most inspired and poetic words ever written were written by David, as the Holy Spirit move upon him.

It was the worshipper in David that caused him to want to restore the Ark of God to His people. However, in his zeal to bring back God's glory, David did not consult the Scriptures to ensure Divine Order.

Borrowing from the World – the New Cart

> **2 Samuel 6:1-4**
> **1 Again David gathered all the choice men of Israel, thirty thousand.**
> **2 And David arose and went with all the people who were with him from Baale Judah to bring up from there the ark of God, whose name is called by the Name, the Lord of Hosts, who dwells between the cherubim.**
> **3 So they set the ark of God on a new cart, and brought it out of the house of Abinadab, which was on the hill; and Uzzah and Ahio, the sons of Abinadab, drove the new cart.**
> **4 And they brought it out of the house of Abinadab, which was on the hill, accompanying the ark of God; and Ahio went before the ark.**

David, in his zeal, brought up the Ark on a new cart. Please remember what we previously covered regarding transporting the Ark. It was to be carried by the priests using staves that went through the gold loops. The priests were to bare it on their shoulders and there was to be no human contact.

Does God give orders without cause? Are His commands really just suggestions? Perhaps there is a better, more modern way of doing it instead of the antiquated way that God prescribed?

No, no and no!

Praise and worship in the house of God is not a frivolous matter. We cannot simply borrow the world's music and add some

Christian lyrics. New Testament divine order is worship in spirit and truth (John 4:24).

Now, there are some in the church who contend that there are a special assortment of songs from a distinct era (in their personal past) that God has chosen to anoint and no others. In other words, some elderly folks only like the old hymns. True praise and worship is not about song style preference.

I have been in the church for over 30 years and I have managed to keep myself close to what God is doing currently in the area of praise and worship. I truly love what God is doing fresh in the area of worship. That is not to say that I don't appreciate the past, but there is something special about the ministry that is proceeding forth from the Throne. Jesus instructed us to be "new wineskins" in order for new wine to be poured into us. If we remain set in "our ways" as "old wineskins" we will burst (Matthew 9:17).

So where did David get this "idea" of transporting the Ark on a new cart? A little bit of reading back into the story quickly reveals that David was simply borrowing from the Philistines – the ungodly.

> **1 Samuel 6:7-8**
> **7 Now therefore, make a new cart, take two milk cows which have never been yoked, and hitch the cows to the cart; and take their calves home, away from them.**
> **8 Then take the ark of the Lord and set it on the cart; and put the articles of gold which you are returning to**

Him as a trespass offering in a chest by its side. Then send it away, and let it go.

David followed the protocol of the Philistines instead of seeking divine order. While God may permit the Philistines and the rest of the heathen world to transport the Ark on a new cart, He does not allow His people to deviate from His Word. Others may… we may not. Perhaps David knew what the Torah said about transporting the Ark, but thought that it longer applied, that it was outdated. This speaks much to today's Church. The Church is borrowing from the world and filling God's House with entertainment.

- Exchanging the Gold for Brass
- Trading the Glory for Gimmicks
- Replacing the Anointing with Hype

It is a sad state of affairs, and even worse, as in Jeremiah's day, God's people love to have it so.

Jeremiah 5:31 The prophets prophesy falsely, And the priests rule by their own power; and My people love to have it so. But what will you do in the end?

God's people are being destroyed for a lack of knowledge (Hosea 4:6). While Moses is on the mount with God, the people of God are partying it up with the golden calf. There is a price for God's glory and divine order must be followed. Entertainment may draw people to attend your Church services, but it will not produce life out of death. The yoke is destroyed because of the Anointing (Isaiah 10:27).

Let's look at this procession of David and the Ark a little closer.

> **2 Samuel 6:5 Then David and all the house of Israel played music before the Lord on all kinds of instruments of fir wood, on harps, on stringed instruments, on tambourines, on sistrums, and on cymbals.**

The worship music was loud and beautiful; it had all of the elements of the "fastest growing churches in America." But there was something missing – it was God's glory, His anointing. I have been in worship gatherings where everything seemed right to the eye and to the ear, but in my spirit, I knew that God was absent. The worship leader was working up the crowd, tapping into the emotions of the people; the preacher was animated and entertaining. But there was no life. No anointing.

The Threshing Floor
A threshing floor was a flat surface that was smooth and hard; it was used to separate the grain from the straw and husks. In order to do this, the mingled harvest had to be beaten manually.

When the procession came to Nachon's threshing floor, there was a shaking that occurred. It is important to know that all that is born of the flesh must be upheld by the flesh. You can't borrow from the world and expect God to anoint and bless.

> **John 3:6 That which is born of the flesh is flesh, and that which is born of the Spirit is spirit.**

John 6:63 It is the Spirit who gives life; the flesh profits nothing. The words that I speak to you are spirit, and they are life.

When the cart with the Ark got to Nachon's threshing floor, there was a shaking. God would not allow the procession to go any further without His divine correction being administered.

2 Samuel 6:6 And when they came to Nachon's threshing floor, Uzzah put out his hand to the ark of God and took hold of it, for the oxen stumbled.

We serve a jealous God. He desires to manifest His presence in our midst, but it must be according to order. Here we see the oxen stumbling and the Ark teetering; Uzzah puts for his hand — the flesh — to steady the Ark because this was all that he could do. Remember, that which originates with the flesh must be carried out by the flesh. God's blessing was not waiting at Nachon's threshing floor.

Conversely, there are a couple of passages in the New Testament that speak to the matter of God's shaking.

Hebrews 12:26-27
26 whose voice then shook the earth; but now He has promised, saying, "Yet once more I shake not only the earth, but also heaven."
27 Now this, "Yet once more," indicates the removal of those things that are being shaken, as of things that are made, that the things which cannot be shaken may remain.

There is an hour of shaking coming upon the earth and it begins in the Church. Only those things that cannot be shaken are going to remain. The entertainment of the modern-day Church will not make it through this time of testing. God is removing those things that can be shaken according to Hebrews 12:27. Just as the new cart began to shake, thereby causing the Ark of God's presence to be jeopardized, God is shaking the Church and purging the works of the flesh from its midst. He is looking for true worshippers (John 4:23).

Both the Old and New Testaments refer to the threshing floor as a symbol of judgment. Hosea prophesied that because Israel had repeatedly turned from God to false idols, His judgment upon them would scatter them to the winds as the chaff from the threshing floor (Hosea 9:2). John the Baptist used the imagery of the threshing floor to describe how Jesus would separate true believers from false ones.

Matthew 3:
9 and do not think to say to yourselves, 'We have Abraham as our father.' For I say to you that God is able to raise up children to Abraham from these stones.
10 And even now the ax is laid to the root of the trees. Therefore every tree which does not bear good fruit is cut down and thrown into the fire.
11 I indeed baptize you with water unto repentance, but He who is coming after me is mightier than I, whose sandals I am not worthy to carry. He will baptize you with the Holy Spirit and fire.

12 His winnowing fan is in His hand, and He will thoroughly clean out His threshing floor, and gather His wheat into the barn; but He will burn up the chaff with unquenchable fire."

John the Baptist was dealing with an attitude of religious pedigree. The Israelites were puffed up with their status as the children of Abraham. He told them that God was able to raise up children to Abraham from stones. God is not impressed with our affiliations and who we have "sat under." John spoke of a baptism with the Holy Spirit and fire. We need to have God's all-consuming presence in our lives today – not stories from yester year.

In verse 12, John speaks of the threshing floor. This is typology for a time of judgment. He said that the one coming after him, Jesus, would have the winnowing fan in His hand. With this fan, He will thoroughly clean His floor. What is His floor? His floor is His house, the Church. The winnowing fan is the Holy Spirit. In this final hour, Jesus will thrust in the fork and toss the harvest into the air. The lighter weighted chaff will be blown away by the fan in His hand and the heavier weighted wheat will drop to the floor, thoroughly cleansed.

The imminence of this is upon us. The fan is already in His hand. God lovingly warns His people to turn to Him, but in obstinance, many harden their hearts. We are at the threshing floor and those who love the Lord desire the cleansing of His house. In the procession found in 2 Samuel chapter 6, the party reached Nachon's threshing floor. The name Nachon means "ready." The time is now.

As the oxen began to stumble, Uzzah put forth his hand to steady the ark, to prevent what he deemed would be catastrophe. But what ensued was the judgment of the Lord against the work of the flesh.

> **2 Samuel 6:**
> **7 Then the anger of the Lord was aroused against Uzzah, and God struck him there for his error; and he died there by the ark of God.**
> **8 And David became angry because of the Lord's outbreak against Uzzah; and he called the name of the place Perez Uzzah to this day.**

God brought judgment upon the proceedings. Uzzah was killed for his error of touching the Ark. God saw presumption and irreverence in Uzzah's heart. He treated the Ark of God's presence with familiarity and without reverence. Remember, Uzzah was a son of Abinidab and the Ark spent 20 years in his house. Many today are flippant with the things of God, making mockery of the work of the Holy Spirit. The threshing floor is coming and the fan is in His hand.

Another lesson to be learned in all this is that no matter who is giving the directions, consult God's Word for yourself. David was sincere, but he was sincerely wrong. One cannot blindly follow a leader under any circumstance. If the Ark of God had not been on a cart, pulled by oxen, this would never have happened. Perhaps Uzzah knew that the Ark should have carried with staves upon the shoulders of the priests, but he did not speak up. The consequence was grave.

1 Peter 4:17 For the time has come for judgment to begin at the house of God; and if it begins with us first, what will be the end of those who do not obey the gospel of God?

Judgment begins with the house of God. In this case, judgment was a means of preserving the sense of God's holiness and the fear of drawing near to Him without appropriate preparation.

The Word says, "David became angry" (v. 8). He couldn't understand why God would bring judgment upon them when he was trying to restore God's glory. Up to this point, David did not have any personal dealings with the Ark of God's presence. He had entered the situation without fully preparing himself. He now realized the gravity of the matter. Verse 9 says, *David was afraid of the Lord that day; and he said, "How can the ark of the Lord come to me?"* David now realized that this matter of restoring God's glory must have preparation and be done according to divine order.

Obededom

> **2 Samuel 6:**
> **10 So David would not move the ark of the Lord with him into the City of David; but David took it aside into the house of Obed-Edom the Gittite.**
> **11 The ark of the Lord remained in the house of Obed-Edom the Gittite three months. And the Lord blessed Obed-Edom and all his household.**

The Ark was moved to Obed-Edom's house and for three months, the Lord blessed Obed-Edom and his entire household. There is blessing in the presence of God. Anyone who wanted the blessing had to go to Obed-Edom's house. For too long, the church has operated this way. Only certain individuals had the blessing. The personal anointings of a select few is not God's divine order. God wants to manifest His presence in His house. While the personal blessing may be at Obed-Edom's house, the corporate anointing is in Zion (Psalm 133). This is where the Ark needed to come.

In the last days, God is pouring His Spirit out on ALL FLESH (Joel 2:28), not just a select few. The days of traveling to see superstar evangelists will be no more. God does not want us having our eyes upon a man.

Through the blessing that was upon Obed-Edom, David was provoked to godly jealousy. After three months of seeking divine order, the time had come to bring back the Ark the right way and set it in its place on the hill of Zion.

The next time that David attempted to restore the Ark to Zion, he did so according to divine order. No more ways of the world. The Ark was transported by the priests, using the staves to carry it upon their shoulders.

The events of this beautiful proceeding are detailed in 2 Samuel 6:12-23 and 1 Chronicles chapters 15 and 16.

As the Ark was ushered into Zion, David danced before the Lord with all his might. In our chapter on HALAL we discuss how David was not concerned about his dignity as the King. One thing about the Tabernacle of David is that there was not an exclusive invitation list. God's presence was available to all worshippers. Even though we was king, in God's presence, David saw himself no better than others.

Shiloh

The tabernacle at Shiloh was still in operation. Nothing had changed. It was business as usual. There was only one problem: the Glory had departed.

Even though the service of the Levites and Priests remained unchanged and sacrifices were still being offered, there was no presence of God. True worship was not in Shiloh, where God had cursed the priesthood of Eli and his sons.

> **Psalm 78:60-61**
> **60 So that He forsook the tabernacle of Shiloh, the tent He had placed among men,**
> **61 And delivered His strength into captivity, and His glory into the enemy's hand.**

This is very representative of today where the organized church continues to function and offer "worship services" but "Ichabod" has been written above the doors because the Glory has departed. But God has a remnant who are finding their place. The Lord is raising up a church in these last days and the Tabernacle of David is being restored – true worship in the presence of God.

The Tent

> **1 Chronicles 15:1 *David* built houses for himself in the City of David; and he prepared a place for the ark of God, and pitched a tent for it.**

The Tabernacle of David was simply a tent pitched in Jerusalem, in Mt. Zion. It housed the Ark of the Covenant until the erection of Solomon's Temple or approximately 40 years. God dwelling with His people in a tent also speaks to the fact that we are sojourners here on the earth as God's children. We are just passing through as pilgrims and strangers.

The procession of the Ark had an arrangement as follows:

- King David (1 Chronicles 15:25)
- The Elders of Israel (1 Chronicles 15:25)
- The Captains of Israel (1 Chronicles 15:25)
- The High Priests (1 Chronicles 15:4-11)
- The Chiefs and Levites (1 Chronicles 15:5-10)

There were trumpeters, doorkeepers, porters, singers, musicians, and all the congregation of Israel following (1 Chronicles 15:12-24).

There were dedicatory sacrifices offered upon the arrival of the Ark to the tent of David. Of course, each of the sacrifices pointed to the Cross – where Jesus became the One and Final Sacrifice for the sins of mankind.

It is of particular interest that after these dedicatory sacrifices there was no further mention of animal sacrifices at the Tabernacle of David. There were, however, sacrifices offered there – ones of praise and worship before the presence of Yahweh.

Tabernacle of Moses - Shiloh	Tabernacle of David - Zion
1. Outer Court and furnishings	1. No Outer Court
2. Holy Place and furnishings	2. No Holy Place
3. Holy of Holies – empty	3. God's Presence in Tent
4. Veil – no access	4. No Veil - access
	5. Ark of the Covenant

5. No Ark of the Covenant 6. Animal Sacrifices - daily	6. Sacrifices of Praise - daily

Under the old Mosaic ministry – per the Law, the Holy of Holies could only be entered once per year by the High Priest. But under the new Davidic ministry, access to the presence of God was always available. This speaks to the New Covenant and the current economy. We may attend to God at any time through the sacrifice of praise and worship in His presence. Hebrews 10:19 tells us that we may enter the throne room with boldness by the blood of Jesus.

In the Tabernacle of David praise and worship was ongoing 24/7. It was a special time in the history of the nation of Israel. Scripture records a variety of ways that ministry occurred in the tent. Kevin Conner, in his wonderful book, "The Tabernacle of David" lists out all of the different ministries in the tent:

1. Ministry of Singers and Singing (1 Chronicles 15:16-27; 25:1-7) (There were never any singers in the Tabernacle of Moses)
2. Ministry of the Musicians with Instruments (1 Chronicles 23:5; 25:1-7) (There were never any instruments in the Tabernacle of Moses)
3. Ministry of Levites before the Ark (1 Chronicles 16:4, 6, 37) (These Levites had access to the Ark of God's presence on a daily basis)
4. Ministry of Recording (1 Chronicles 16:4; 28:12, 19) (Many of the 150 Psalms were uttered in the tent and recorded)
5. Ministry of Thanking the Lord (1 Chronicles 16:4, 8, 41) (Unthankfulness is an earmark of the end times. Thankfulness, by contrast, is an earmark of the Church)

6. Ministry of Praise (1 Chronicles 16:4, 36) (Praises were both spoken and sang in the tent)
7. Ministry of Psalms (1 Chronicles 16:9; Psalm 98:6) (The majority of the Psalms are linked to David's Tabernacle)
8. Ministry of Rejoicing and Joy (1 Chronicles 16:10, 16, 25-31) (The Tabernacle of Moses was characterized by solemnity but the Tabernacle of David by joy)
9. Ministry of Clapping of Hands (Psalm 47:1; 98:8; Isaiah 55:12) (A natural human response to the goodness of God)
10. Ministry of Shouting (1 Chronicles 15:28; Psalm 47:1, 5; Isaiah 12:6) (There was much shouting when the Ark was restored and throughout its time in the tent)
11. Ministry of Dancing (1 Chronicles 15:29; 2 Samuel 6:14; Psalm 149:3; 150:4) (David's example speaks volumes)
12. Ministry of Lifting up of Hands (Psalm 134; 141:2) (The lifting of hands was the evening sacrifice – Psalm 141:2)
13. Ministry of Worship (1 Chronicles 16:29; Psalm 29:1-2; 95:6) (Praise is our response to God's goodness and worship is our response to God's presence)
14. Ministry of Seeking the Lord (1 Chronicles 16:29; Psalm 29:1-2; 95:6) (God's face was sought in the tent)
15. Ministry of Spiritual Sacrifices (Psalm 27:6; 1 Peter 2:3-5; Hebrews 13:15-16) (Only the dedicatory sacrifices were offered – all else were spiritual sacrifices)
16. Ministry of Saying "Amen" (1 Chronicles 16:36) (The "amen" of God's blessing)

If these ministries sound a lot like the seven Hebrew words for "praise," it is no coincidence. This is the order of praise and worship that God is restoring to the Church of God in the end times.

God never again returned to Shiloh. What was done was done. Just as Jesus said, "Let the dead bury their dead; follow Me" (Luke 9:59-60). There are millions of people still in churches that are dead and dry. Perhaps they remain for different reasons. It could be that's where they were raised, where their family had always gone. Possibly, it's a sense of loyalty or even guilt. Whatever the reason, Jesus still says, "Follow Me."

There is a reason that the Word of God tells us that we are come unto Mount Zion (Hebrews 12:22). The religious legalism of Mount Sinai is dead.

If the true praise and worship of the Tabernacle of David has not been restored to your local church and instead you see the ways of the world and political correctness taking over, run. Run! Find a church where an encounter with God is still a regular activity.

QUESTIONS

1. What did the Ark of the Covenant represent?

2. What does a Threshing Floor symbolize in Scripture?

3. As it relates to animal sacrifices, explain the difference between the Tabernacle of Moses and the Tabernacle of David:

4. List at least five ministries of the Tabernacle of David in which you participate:

The Secret Place

Pure Heart

A pure heart in worship is one that is without secret agenda and is free from ulterior motives. To worship God without an agenda centers on seeking God's face (Who He is) and not His hand (what He does). There is a time to ask God for His blessing and seek Him for what He does, but worship is not that time. Standing in His presence is a time of intimacy when nothing is asked for except more of Him.

In Worship we seek God's face and not His hand

His Face	His Hand
Who He is	What He does

We looked at Psalm 24 in the chapter on Our Highest Calling. Let's read it again.

Psalm 24:3-4
3 Who may ascend into the hill of the Lord?
Or who may stand in His holy place?
4 He who has clean hands and a pure heart
Who has not lifted up his soul to an idol...

Notice that David spoke about not lifting your soul up to an idol. An idol is anything in our lives that takes the place of God in our priorities. Idolatry will prevent a believer from enjoying the fullness of God's manifest presence.

Matthew 5:8 The pure in heart shall see God.

Hebrews 12:14 Without holiness no one will see the Lord

What does it mean to have a pure heart when it comes to worship? How can one do introspection to examine his heart if he is unclear what it means to have a pure heart? Purity differs from Holiness. In its simplest form, to be *pure* means "to be free from mixture," but to be *holy* means "to be free from contamination."

Pure = Free from Mixture
Holy = Free from Contamination

To see God in worship, our hearts need to be pure – free from mixture, meaning an undivided heart. True worship requires singular focus. Once we have removed the contamination (i.e., the sin) out of our lives (through the work of the cross), our attention should be on giving God our undivided attention in worship.

Enter the Secret Place and Close the Door
Worship is an intimate experience between a child of God and the Heavenly Father. Jesus taught the importance of entering a secret place when spending time with God.

Matthew 6:6
But you, when you pray, go into your room, and when you have shut your door, pray to your Father who is in the secret place; and your Father who sees in secret will reward you openly.

The Greek word used for "room" is also translated "secret chamber" in Matthew 24:26. Jesus is not speaking of a literal room, closet or secret chamber, but one of the heart. Even in a crowded worship service, you can enter into the secret place. It is the same place spoken of in Psalm 91 ("He who dwells in the secret place of the Most High shall abide under the shadow of the Almighty").

Jesus also said that after you enter into the secret place to shut the door. What does it mean to shut the door? There are so many potential distractions that can steal our focus. Satan is the master of distractions. The last thing he wants is true worship of the Heavenly Father. The enemy doesn't mind good music, lifting hands, and all the other outward forms of worship, but when a believer's heart connects with God in true worship in spirit and truth, he knows that life-changing power from God has dispelled him.

Worship requires singular focus on God. In today's world, there are constant multiple inputs vying for our attention. At work, it is multi-tasking all day long, every day. The days of focusing on one project are over. The weekends are overbooked with events with the kids and grandkids and non-stop activities. Sunday rolls around and on the drive to church, the driver is listening to the radio, drinking a cup of coffee, holding a conversation and texting... at the same time. When he enters the sanctuary for worship, it can be the hardest thing to enter the secret place and shut the door. This is why we must condition ourselves to the secret place. Spending time with God alone prepares us for spending time with Him in a public worship meeting.

Worship requires Singular Focus on God
But we are Programmed for Multiple Channels of Input

When we truly "lock in" with our worship in our meetings, in one accord, the manifest presence of God is going to be revealed and the miraculous will begin to flow.

When we HALAL or BARAK it will not be in the outward show of the flesh, but an expression of the life of the Spirit in us.

QUESTIONS

1. Explain the difference between God's face and God's hand:

2. What is the difference between holiness and purity?

3. What is the biggest hindrance in your life to entering the secret place?

Other books by David Chapman

Blood Covenant

The Believer's Deliverance Handbook

The Fullness of the Spirit

Modern Day Apostles

The Pattern and the Glory

Thus Saith The Lord

The Power of the Anointing

Knowing God's Will

Caught Up: The Rapture of the Church